JAGGED RHYTHMS

Carol Battaglia

A Nurse Owned Company

√ISTA
Publishing, Inc.

Copyright © 1997 by Carol Battaglia

Edited by Carolyn S. Zagury, RN, MS, CPC

Cover Design and art work by Thomas Taylor of Thomcatt Graphics

A special thanks to Russell Gordon, Zuma Press for the author's cover photo.

Vista Publishing, Inc.
473 Broadway
Long Branch, NJ 07740
(908) 229-6500

This publication has been designed and written for the reading pleasure of the general public. All references to people, places and situations are fictional and in no way intended to depict actual people, places or situations.

Printed and bound in the United States of America

First Edition

ISBN: 1-880254-45-X

Library of Congress Catalog Card Number: 97-60581

USA Price $12.95
Canada Price $16.95

DEDICATION

To Jack with love and gratitude.

To my friends for their healing powers.

To my colleagues in the Medicine Subspecialty section at Loyola who taught me what it was like to feel like a nurse again.

To Dorothy and Mary, who read the stories with open hearts.

To Dr. William Hopkinson, orthopedic surgeon at Loyola University Medical Center, for his gifts of mobility and hope.

And lastly to Carolyn Zagury and the people at Vista Publishing, Inc. who continue to provide an avenue for release.

Thanks everyone.

If we are lucky,
one day we awake
and realize that
we are not alone.

Carol Battaglia

Meet The Author

I first met Carol Battaglia twenty five years ago in an outpatient clinic where her literary skills where hidden by a starched, white uniform. Carol is currently a Nurse Practitioner at Loyola University Medical Center in Maywood, Illinois. She has worked in the county hospital, on an Indian Reservation and at university medical centers. Carol's experiences unfold in her writing generating poems and stories that unveil the human spirit of those caring for the sick or being cared for. In her writings she allows the heart to bleed the words that characterize the nursing forces for caring, healing, suffering and comforting - when nothing else prevails.

Reading this work provokes *Jagged Rhythms* in the mind which ignite those energies that allow us to endure, to survive the repetitive daily activities, to reflect on our frailties or illnesses, and to enjoy the honor to serve those that need us.

Carol Battaglia's clinical expertise modulated by her insight, spirituality and sensitivity that are seen in her "proetry", as she calls it, along with a whimsical point of view have made her a colleague of immeasurable value and a source of inspiration to the nursing profession.

Jessie E. Hano, M.D.
Professor of Medicine
Director, Division of Renal Disease
& Hypertension
Loyola University Medical Center

Special Thoughts About *Jagged Rhythms* ...

"At a time when the timeless profession of medicine is being transformed into "health care industry" it is gratifying and refreshing to read this collection of poems and vignettes. This anthology clearly speaks to the timelessness of the healing arts and identifies that it encompasses not only the profession of medicine, nursing and its associated care givers, but also underscores the importance of ministry of all denominations and perspectives as essential to the process.

The essence of the message is captured in the *Margin*, "The only thing that separates us is that I have not yet been diagnosed." To have had and continue to have the opportunity of caring for patients with Carol Battaglia is a blessing that is difficult to articulate, lacking her literary skills."

Leonard L. Vertuno, MD
Professor of Medicine,
Louola Univeristy Medical Center

"We are fortunate to have Carol Battaglia appear on our literary horizon. Writing from the edges of both nurse and patient she is able to articulate with luminous clarity our innermost thoughts, bringing to the surface visions and dreams we only dared muse about.

In *Jagged Rhythms* the humdrum of a nurses' life is exposed, but in it being laid bare considerable richness is unveiled. The giftedness of Battaglia is to probe deeply to discover new value and treasure. In all this she engages us personally without allowing her style to become self-conscious.

As seen from her earlier writings, Battaglia can touch those cords of the heart to which we give only meager attention. In her poetry and stories these is pathos that begs for tenderness, frailty that seeks strengthening, forgiveness, and joy waiting to be exuberantly celebrated."

Rev. Bede Jagoe, O.P.

"The author captures the feelings of both patient and nurse from each one's perspective - you can easily uncover the essence of the "night nurse" tending the sick in those dark hours."

Nancy Vertuno, RN

INTRODUCTION

This is a book of poems and stories, reflections on hospital life and of being ill and of coming back from a state of disease. The first section sees things from the standpoint of the nurse as she/he wades through the day. The second part looks at life on the other side of the bed rails, where the patient lives and struggles.

When I first began to compile the poems, to place them on their respective pages. I was struck by their dysrhythmia. I noted that they did not possess the flow of my earlier work, poems that were not about nursing or illness. I thought then that perhaps I had lost some inner cadence, some ability to record rhythm. But then I realized that the sometimes jagged rhythm is what our nursing life is all about.

We are constantly interrupted by requests that affect the flow of what we are doing. We stop and start, change direction, move in and out of many people's lives throughout the day.

We experience happiness and sadness. We are stressed, worried and sometimes angry. We are being reorganized. restructured, and down staffed. And through it all we are expected to smile while bearing the weight of burdens that eventually take their toll. We burn out, we crash and we rise again to face another day.

My jagged poems arise from that experience. They do not flow harmoniously across the page, but then neither do we.

Table of Contents

Nursing Rhythms

Table of Contents

Section One

Nursing Rhythms

Night Visitor

"Come on Bridgette, I've got to have some help up here. There has got to be someone that you can send. I have an 85 year old lady who keeps screaming for me, believing that I am her mother. Every time I go in to her room she gets me in this death-like grasp pleading for me not to leave her alone.

Then there is this alcoholic who thinks that he is a United States senator late for a cabinet meeting. He keeps yelling. "The President won't like this, you are holding me against my will." He is threatening to call the FBI, for God's sake. I had to take the phone out of his room.

I have a GI bleeder whose pressure is going down, and a new intern on service who has barricaded himself in the break room with the *Washington Manual*, reading as fast as he can."

"Bridge, it is only 2 a.m. I'm never going to make it till the end of the shift." I listened on the phone as Bridgette, the night nursing supervisor, said that she "got the message", and that she would check around to see if any of the units had someone to spare. She hung up before I could get some zingers in about what I thought about the "new model of care". This grand plan that down sizes nursing personnel saving the hospital money, but wearing out the nurses left behind. I'm getting too old for this, I reminded myself for the hundredth time this year.

My thoughts were interrupted by the shrill cry of, "Mama. Mama", coming from the old lady's room. "I'll be right there my darling." I called back. Two could play at this game, I thought.

I passed the break room and saw that the intern was on his fourth cup of coffee, and wasn't showing any signs of emerging soon. Great, I told myself, he will probably develop palpitations from all that caffeine and I will end up taking care of him. Now he had *Harrison's* text of medicine and the *Washington Manual* in front of him. "What could he be looking up?" I asked myself.

I checked on the bleeder as I made my way down to my 85 year old daughter. The blood was running, thank God, and he was sleeping. Well, at first glance I thought that he was asleep, but as I checked his pressure I realized that he was probably going into shock. While yelling for the intern. I opened the saline line and placed the bed in shock position. The intern came flying in to the room, took one look at the patient and passed out. "Oh this is really great!" I said to my two senseless companions. "Just what I needed." I ran in to the bathroom, filled a glass with water, tripped coming out of the bathroom and landed on the intern. The water ended up on his face and he sputtered back in to consciousness.

He appeared to be a little surprised that I was laying across his chest. "I'm OK", he said, "Just a little hypoglycemic. I haven't eaten all day and I think that I might have had too much coffee." I untangled myself from his body and told him that I would get him something to eat. First I checked the patient's blood pressure and was relieved to see that it was coming up. I went down to the fridge and pulled out my cheese sandwich and a carton of milk. I put some sugar in a can of orange juice and brought it back to the intern, who was still on the floor, but sitting now propped against the wall. "Here eat." I commanded. "This should do the trick."

"Thanks, I'm a little shaky. How's the bleeder?" he asked.

"Pressures up, but you will have to stay with him while I check on the senator and the old gal down the hall."

"No problem, I'm feeling much better. I can do this."

"I know you can." I replied. "Want me to get your books?" He gave me a forlorn look and I apologized saying that it was the pressure talking. As I left the room I noticed that he had a piece of cheese stuck to his cheek. I smiled, but did not say anything because it was the first time that I had had something to smile about since my shift began.

"Mama, Mama!" the old lady's voice grew louder. "Coming my little liebschen." I yelled back.

"Men, I'm in here." the senator called out. "Now they have my secretary trapped in the next room." he continued. "Call the President, we have to get out of here, the Cabinet is awaiting our presentation."

"What a night!" I said to no one in particular. As I made my way down the darkened hospital hall, the elevator door opened and a small figure stepped out. She was dressed in nursing white and looked quite pale. Her dark hair touched her shoulders and billowed out as she came towards me.

"I am here to help." she said in a calming voice.

"Hallelujah', I replied. "Let's stop at the desk, and I will fill you in on the inhabitants of this madhouse."

She followed me in to the nursing station. I introduced myself, and she said that her name was Mary. She looked kind of fragile, waif-like really, and I hoped that she would be able to make it through the shift. She said that she had not worked in a while, but that she loved working on the floors and that she had really missed taking care of patients.

2

"Well, you should get your fill tonight." I replied. I filled Mary in on the cast of characters, including the intern with the cheese on his face.

My report was interrupted by a call from the emergency room saying that they were sending up a guy in Congestive Heart Failure. I was writing down his orders when the shrill cry of "Mama" resonated down the hall.

"I'll take care of it." Mary said as she floated out of the nursing station.

"Watch her grip." I told Mary. "She has the strength of an iron worker." I said a small prayer of thanks to a God that I wasn't sure was there and returned to the phone.

When I was finished talking to the emergency room nurse. I walked down the hall to check on the GI bleeder and the intern. "How are you doing?" I asked the cheese faced intern.

"I think he's stabilizing, his blood pressure is up and his pulse rate is normal. He seems to be coming out of it." I told him that that was great news and then filled him in on the new admission.

"The ER Doc said that the guy was not in any acute distress. From what he told me the patient loves pickles, ate four of them today and tipped over in to heart failure. He said that they gave him a lot of Lasix and that he will probably be peeing all night. I'll call you when he hits the floor."

As I continued my way down the hall I had the feeling that something was different. Something that I couldn't quite put my finger on. Then I got it! It was quiet, with only the soft murmur of voices coming from the senator's room. I approached cautiously and was rewarded with my second laugh of the night. Mary had moved Mrs. Casey, the 85 year old, into the senator's room. She sat secured in a wheel chair next to his bed and was holding his hand. The senator was saying that he was glad his secretary had finally come and that they had a lot of work to do. Mrs. Casey whispered to me, over toothless gums, that she wasn't really his secretary. She said that he was her son and that he was sick, and that she would like to stay with him.

"That would be fine Mrs. Casey, just call out if you need us." Whatever it takes, I told myself as I left the room and them to their delusions.

I searched for Mary, and finally found her in Mrs. Lincoln's room. Mrs. Lincoln was dying and not expected to make it through the night. I stood in the door way and watched as Mary whispered in to the dying woman's ear. I heard her say, "Oh child of noble family, listen without distraction." I could not hear what followed, but then heard her repeat the phrase again. Puzzled, I glanced at Mrs. Lincoln's face and was amazed to see a soft glow emanating through her skin. Mary saw me, and came to where I was standing. "It won't be long now." she said. "She's almost there." Sensing my confusion she went on to explain that Mrs.

3

Lincoln was at the "bardo of the moment before death." The way she explained it was that the Buddhists believed that this was a time of detachment of the person's consciousness from the world in which they find themselves, and a preparation for their journey into the next life. She told me that the words she spoke to Mrs. Lincoln were from something called *THE TIBETAN BOOK OF THE DEAD*", and that they were meant to guide the spirit of the person at this time of transmigration.

I stared at Mary for a moment. And for one brief second I thought that I understood what she was talking about. But then it was gone. Then I said. "Say what?" But before she could answer we were interrupted by the arrival of "Pickle Man", the guy from the emergency room in heart failure. The ER technician rolled him down the hall announcing "special delivery".

"Cute Fredie." I said, "just help us get him in to bed."

The patient, Mr. Buffo, was a smallish Italian man that appeared to be carrying about 10 pounds of extra fluid in his body tissues. Mary and I worked to settle him comfortably, and then I left her to finish the task of admitting him to the unit. As I went to get the intern. I thought about how much help Mary had been this night. And about how one felt calmer in her presence, less harried. I was not sure about all that Tibetan stuff, but I did know that just having her around was a comfort.

I went in to the GI bleeders room, and stopped for a moment and watched Charlie, the intern with the cheese still on his face, work his way expertly over the patient. "How are things?" I asked.

"Great." he replied. "The second unit of blood went in without a hitch and his vital signs are stable. He woke up once, gave me a strange look, and then went back to sleep. Wonder what that was all about?"

"Couldn't say." I replied. But when you're finished in here have a look at the guy that came up from the ER. I think that he needs more Lasix."

"Be there in a minute." Charlie said in a doctorly manner. I told myself that I was going to have to tell him about that cheese on his face. But I went to answer the phone in the nursing station instead. On my way to the ringing phone, I checked on Mrs. Casey and the senator. They were both asleep, and they were still holding hands. I thought that reality could wait, and I quietly left the room.

After answering the phone. I made my way down the hall to check on Mary and Mr. Buffo. I found her speaking to him in soothing tones. His breathing was less labored, and he appeared quite relaxed. At this point Charlie came in and went about the business of assessing the patient. Mr. Buffo opened one eye, looked at the intern, and said "Doc you know what goes good with a cheese sandwich? A big salty pickle!"

4

"Just relax Mr. Buffo you are in the hospital. Where do they come up with this stuff?" Charlie asked me.

"Beats me." I replied. I grabbed a tissue and told Charlie, while wiping the cheese from his face, that he had a big spot of ink on his cheek.

"Thanks, I wouldn't want to appear unprofessional." Mr. Buffo looked at us as if we were crazy and then closed his eyes.

Mary and I left the room smiling. We spent the next hour working together completing all the tasks of the night nurse as the shift winds down. We put Mrs. Casey back to bed, and left her sleeping peacefully. I watched Mary work and admired her tender touch. Being around her helped me remember my early years in nursing. Those years when caring merged with skill and made me glad to be at the bedside.

"I have to go now. I don't think that I can stay any longer." Mary said.

"Thanks for all your help, Mary. I would not have made it through this night without you."

"The gods watch over night nurses." she replied. "We are like shepherds in the night fields, trying to shield our flock from harm." Saying that she lightly grasped my hand, turned and disappeared down the darkened corridor.

I watched as she entered the waiting elevator and then went in to the nursing station to answer the phone. It was Bridgette, the night supervisor. "Sorry that I wasn't able to find you anyone." she said. "We had an emergency on the fourth floor. It was pretty sad, really." she continued. "Mary Rogers, a patient who was a nurse, had a cardiac arrest. We worked on her for a couple of hours, but just couldn't bring her back. She just kept slipping away from us. It's too bad. I heard that she was a nice person, and good nurse."

Stunned I stared at the phone in disbelief, then finally found my voice. "Yes she was." I replied. "Yes she was." I repeated, as I slowly hung up the phone.

Aegis

This uniform,
this barricade of white
I hope that it endures.

Ethereal Jam

Sometimes,
it takes all my strength
to push against
the spirits of the dead,
stacked, trapped
in the corridors
of the living.

Sacrificium

My colleagues,
my sisters,
cloaked in bride-like
white.
Visions of virginal
offerings come to mind.

Substitution

Today, instead
of pills, I am
passing out
mantras.

Audible Steps

Patients never see my shoes.
I think I'll paint them red,
and fasten taps to their soles.
Then they could chart my course,
know that I am near.
Tap--Tap--Tap--
Wouldn't that be fun?

A Secret

"They" pay me for
what comes naturally --
nurturing, but I'll
never tell.

The Gamble

If I touch you
I risk knowing you.
Oh! What the hell!

Thin Margin

The only thing
that separates us
is that I have not
yet been diagnosed.

Evanesce

We have taken your clothes,
the cloths that preserve
your identity.
Now, dressed in worn
costumes of hospital
gowns, you begin to fade
into the bed sheets,
and slowly ever so slowly
disappear.

Freight

Hospital regatta,
sailing vessels of
live cargo.
White sheet sails,
transporters at the helm,
these captains seeking
a safe port.

Best Laid Plans

It had all the makings of a good night. The census was down, the remaining patients were stable, and it was the first Friday of the month, our costume party night.

The four of us, Beverly the other RN, Margaret the LPN, Jamil Jones our orderly, and myself had worked together for several years. We not only liked each other and got on well, but we respected the importance of our various levels of practice. We knew that we could count on one another to get the job done and make it through the night shift that linked our lives together.

About three months ago we devised our "costume night". The rules were pretty simple. You could attach a small object to your person or wear something, not too conspicuous, as your costume. Then, the others would have to guess who or what you were. The game kept us amused during the long hours of our shift. We would start about 1 a.m. when we knew that the night supervisor was in her office wading through the ton of paper work that she never seemed to quite finish. We thought that she would probably not be amused with our little game, and so we took great pains to keep the secret among us.

We were a competitive lot, each one wanting to emerge the winner the one with the costume that the other three could not guess. Margaret never won, of course. She was a petite pretty girl with massive amounts of dark brown hair. She always picked something "cute". Like the time she taped bows to her uniform and wore a sticker of a little bird. "Little Bow Peep," we yelled in unison as soon as she stepped out of the medicine room. "Damn, you guys think that you are so smart. One of these days I am going to win this game!" We looked at each other and mouthed the words "fat chance" to her retreating back.

Anyway, on the night that this story is about we had finished checking on our respective patients and failing to identify any major problems we separated to attach our costume paraphernalia. I was sure that I would win that night. I had taped a small rock to my shoulder. I was Sisyphus, the Greek mythological figure who had angered the gods and was thereby doomed to roll this heavy rock up a hill for eternity. I was pretty confident that the three numskulls would not be able to figure that out. I went in to the nursing station and there was Margaret with her hair braided and wearing a pair of red tennis shoes. What a simp. I thought, she's Dorothy from the Wizard of Oz. Jamil walked in with a medicine bottle taped to his shoulder. Hmmm, this was going to take some thought.

"Guess away Hommes." Jamil said. "I be the winner tonight!" I always got a kick out of Jamil when he reverted to what he called "hood talk". He was an articulate black man who worked nights as an orderly while finishing his accounting degree. He would leave us soon, and although we were happy for him, we were sad at the prospect of loosing him.

So there we all sat in the nursing station. Jamil with the medicine bottle on his shoulder, Margaret with her red shoes and braided hair, and me and my rock, waiting for Beverly to make her grand entrance. Beverly was a tall, mahogany colored, black woman, who possessed great tenderness. I liked to watch Bev and Margaret work together. Margaret came up to Bev's chest, and was as pale as Bev was dark, and yet they worked in a harmonious rhythm like some mismatched twins complimenting each other.

The door to the break room finally opened, and we collapsed in laughter as Beverly stepped out. Her head was tightly bound in a colorful scarf, making her face appear yards wide. And around her waist was fastened a checkered apron. "Aunt Jemima!" we managed to get out amid peals of laughter.

"If any of the sisters see me, I'm dead meat!" Beverly said. What Beverly was referring to was that she was known for her strong stance on the rights of black women. She worked relentlessly to point out stereotypical attitudes that defined the black woman in our society, and was looked upon as a leader within the hospital community. That is why we thought her choice of a costume so hilarious.

Now, if you will remember at the beginning of this story I said that this should have been a good night. My mistake in stating that assumption was not remembering one of the classic rules of nursing. Which is never, never under any circumstances say or imply that the shift looked like it was going to go smoothly. Because the very act of announcing this awakens forces that once unleashed are determined to prove you wrong. That was when we began to smell the smoke!

"What's that smell?" Jamil asked. My reply was cut short by the blaring of the fire alarm. And then the hospital operator came on the overhead page and announced *"Mister RED first floor, south wing!"*

"That's right below us." Beverly said in a voice attempting to control panic. We ran out of the nursing station and saw a thin layer of smoke rising from under the south stairwell door. Beverly and Margaret headed down the south corridor to evacuate the patients across from the stairwell. The smoke was heavier there and they were soon forced to crawl on their hands and knees. Jamil appeared with watered down towels and began closing the doors to the patient's rooms and placing the wet towels under them to keep the smoke out. I ran to check the north staircase realizing that it would be our only avenue of escape. The door leading to the north stairs was cool to touch. I stepped to the side, and cracked the door open cautiously. The air was clear and free of smoke. *Thank God!, I* thought.

The hall phone rang. I picked it up and heard the voice of the night supervisor instructing me to move the patients off the unit. "Can we use the north stairwell?" I asked.

"Yes, it's safe ....," she began. And then the phone went dead.

As I ran down the hall to find the others, I could hear the sirens of approaching fire engines. The magnitude of the sound increased my fear, and I wondered if we were going to make it through this. I saw Beverly and Margaret coming towards me. They had wrapped the two little old ladies from the end rooms in blankets, and were pulling them down the hall. Jamil was behind them checking all the rooms down the south corridor to make sure that they were empty. We crawled along the hall under the smoke line, and I filled them in on the plan to evacuate the patients. "It's a good thing that we are not full, and that most of the patients are in the north wing." I said.

We finally made it to the end of the north hall where the air was clearer and free of smoke. Able to stand now, we parked the blanketed patients against the wall, and began to rouse the sleeping patients and escort them from their rooms. Jamil lead them down the stairs and Margaret positioned herself at the rear of the descending frightened column. Beverly and I stayed behind with the two patients that were unable to walk. Jamil shouted that he would be right back with help.

Beverly and I checked the mummy wrapped patients, and told them not to be afraid, that everything was going to be OK. Mrs. Fister, the ninety year old, kept staring at Beverly. It was then that I realized that in all the excitement we had forgotten to take off our costumes. So, there sat Beverly in her Aunt Jemima get-up, cradling Mrs. Fister in her arms. I began to laugh. "What's so funny?" Beverly asked.

"You should see yourself." I replied. "You look like Mammy from *Gone With The Wind!*"

"Well, at least I don't have no stupid rock taped to my shoulder. Who are you supposed to be anyway?" she asked.

"It's a long story." I said. Just then Jamil and Margaret came back up the stairway followed by two firemen. They picked up the patients and escorted us down the stairs to safety. We emerged in to the cool morning air, filled our lungs with the freshness of it, and then made our way over to where the patients were huddled. Having satisfied ourselves that everyone was accounted for, we helped

18

the firemen load the patients into waiting ambulances. They were being taken to St. Mary's hospital a few miles away. They were frightened and somewhat bewildered, so we assured them that we would be checking on them latter in the day.

"What a night!" Jamil said. Margaret started to speak, but was interrupted by a TV reporter from a local station. The four of us stood there captured in the television lights. Margaret with her braided hair and red shoes. Bev in her scarf and apron. Jamil with the medicine bottle, and me and my rock. We must have been quite a sight! Reporters were firing questions at us about the fire and our escape. They said that we were heroes, and that our picture and story would be in all the papers.

Beverly slowly moved her hand up to her head, and trying not to call attention to herself removed the scarf that bound her hair. She should have left it on, because now her hair was matted down on the sides but stood straight up on top! At this point the night supervisor appeared and rescued us from the reporters. She took one look at us and said. "I don't even want to know, spare me the details. We will talk about it tomorrow."

Our story was on the afternoon news and in the evening papers. And we spent the next month being both congratulated and ribbed by our coworkers. Time passed and we eventually went our separate ways. Beverly was awarded a scholarship and completed her Masters degree. Margaret took up interior design, at which she was a huge success. And Jamil went on to become a very good accountant. I stayed on, but it was never the same without the other three. We have kept in touch over the years, bound by our friendship and by the memory of that night.

Oh, and by the way, in case you are wondering about Jamil's custom, he was supposed to be a "Medicine Man". Get it? Medicine bottle, taped to his shoulder. Well, I guess that you had to be there.

The Burden

It is the end of my shift.
I look down and see a drop
of your blood on my uniform.

I realize that I have carried
you with me all these long hours.
No wonder I am so worn out.

Sustenance

Sometimes,
the only nourishment
available is in the
hospital cafeteria.
What a horrendous thought!

Deleted

You're smiling today
I'm glad.
Things are not so
hot for me.
I am forbidden to show you myself.
This uniform shields
you from my trouble.
You have enough to bear.

But, it is strange
that our intimate
relationship does not
include any knowledge
of me.

The Visit

Here come the visitors
bringing gifts and news
of the outside world.
They approach with
awkwardness, not sure
of their position.
False smiles worn to
cover their worry.

Missing In Action

Jesus is missing
from the cross
in your room.
I think He has
gone "a visiting".

Restoration

I would like to
wheel you down to the nursery, for
some renewal.
So that you might
feel the strength
of new life,
experience hope.
But, it is not
allowed.

Coalescence

Ministering to your needs,
I forget my own.
With the folding of your
bed corners, I tuck myself
neatly into your world.

Beyond the Flow Sheet

Charts,
chronicles of illness.
No space on the flow sheet
to grade your courage,
record your valor.

Resilience

Stretched beyond belief.
I feel like that ball at
the end of a paddle,
always bouncing back
after each hit.

Trail of Tears

Rounding doctors,
passing out sentences
judge-like.
Trailing nurses,
cleaning up the debris.
Who wipes her tears?

A Plea

Nurses changing shifts,
relay runners handing
over the baton.
Please, don't let me
be the one to drop it!

Alternatives

If it were up to me
I would fill the corridors
with priests and monks
and shamans, and just
let things happen.

Unused

New nurses,
new recruits,
fresh souls to
fight this battle.

Waddle

Medical students
on rounds.
Images of baby ducks
leap to mind.

Weighted Conveyance

Hospital elevators
are burdened with more
than just physical weight.
They carry hope, grief,
relief, help --

Is it any wonder that
they are so slow.

Pathos

My fingers gently close your eyes
not wanting your spirit tempted
with the sight of this world.
Take me with you, I want to say.
I am so very tired.
Maybe, I'll just have a coke.

Higher Plans

I sat in morning report in that half-alert state so familiar to most nurses that work the day shift. That mode of being where one part of the brain is poised for action positioned to respond, while the remaining brain sleepily awakens. I took a big gulp of my morning coffee and attempted to concentrate on what Sally the night nurse was saying, because I simply could not believe what I was hearing.

"Now let me get this straight, Sal. There is a Navajo medicine man in 02, a Buddhist monk in 04, a Jesuit priest in 06, a Catholic nun in 08, and two Rabbis in 10."

"You got it!" Sally replied. "Apparently there is some kind of spiritual awakening seminar in town, and our lot was on a bus that got hit on the expressway. They put the Baptist ministers on the third floor, and I understand that there are still a few fundamentalist in the ER attempting to "save" the staff down there. The injuries on our guys are minor, but administration thought that it would be a good idea if they were admitted for 23 hour observation. I've scheduled the x-rays that were ordered, and the Jesuit's CT scan for mid morning. Have fun! Oh. I forgot to mention one thing. They seem to have a thing about using their call lights. So you have to keep checking to see if they are OK. I think that they don't want to bother us or take us away from others that might need some attention. It's pretty interesting really." Sally concluded.

"Yeah, interesting to you Sal. You're on your way home. I'm left here with this spiritual smorgasbord, and I am an agnostic for God's sake. Did I really say that? I asked myself. Their energies are working on me already, I thought.

I finished my coffee, armed myself with my clipboard, and headed down the hall. OK, first stop the Navajo. "Good morning Mr. Yazzi. My name is Grace, I'll be your nurse today."

"Yes I know." he replied. I've been waiting for you."

Oh, so it's going to be like that is it, I thought. A day of operating on higher planes, one in which my movements are known to others before me.

"Sally told me that you would be coming. I think my IV is almost finished."

"Sally told you.", I replied. "I thought ... well, never mind what I thought, let's have a look." I busied myself with examining the IV and connecting the second bag of intravenous fluids. Get a grip. I told myself. Relax. "This should do it for a while." I said. I fussed with his pillows, and straightened his bed. All the while taking note of his long pony tail, and of the beautiful turquoise necklace that hung around his neck. He had this marvelous craggy face burnt from many summers. The kind of face on which stories were written, a face that spoke of living a life that had not always been easy.

"How's your wrist?" Mr. Yazzi asked me.

"It's better." I replied. "I ... wait a minute, how did you know about my wrist?" He did not answer, but asked instead if he could see my hand. I offered him my left wrist with some trepidation. I had injured it yesterday carrying a load of dirt for the garden. He cupped his big hands around my wrist, and at first I felt a soothing coolness. But then a sensation of warmth began to penetrate the soreness alleviating much of the discomfort. I looked up from his hands to search his face for some understanding of what had just happened. His eyes were closed, but then slowly opened and gazed in to mine. I could not read what I saw there, it was something old and foreign to me and so I looked away in some confusion and stammered a tongue tied "Thanks". "Is there anything that I can do for you?" I asked as I pulled my hand away.

"No. I'm fine. I would like to leave soon. Is that possible?"

"The doctors should be around in an hour or so." I told him. "Then we will see about getting you out of here."

"Thanks", I'm not very comfortable in hospitals." he concluded.

With that I left him, and once outside his room I leaned against the wall attempting to regain my composure. Was that strange, or what? I asked myself. I took several deep breaths, and trying to pull myself together, I headed in to the next room, the room of the Buddhist monk.

"Good morning Reverend Lert, my name is Grace and I'm your nurse today.

"Yes I know." he replied.

"Sally must have told you that I would be around." I said.

"No." he quietly answered. I inspected his face and found that it was as smooth as Mr. Yazzi's was rough. It looked polished and kind of glowed. It was the kind of face that told nothing, gave one no hint of what its wearer was thinking. It was a face that guarded secrets well.

"Let me check the cut on your head." I asked the face. I unwound the bandage that encircled his bald head, and lifted the gauze that covered the laceration. I stared in amazement at a wound almost healed! "This is unbelievable Reverend I can barely tell where your injury was."

"The unbelievable is within our grasp." he began. "If we step beyond ourselves and break through our perceptions of how things should proceed, then all is possible." he concluded.

"But Reverend Lert the wound appears days old instead of hours."

"There is no time. There is just now and the order of the moment." he countered. "For example," he went on, "I sense that you are troubled about something in the future. You are worried about how things will turn out. But your worry does nothing to shape the outcome. It is fruitless. It bears nothing. It serves only to distract you from the moment in which you find yourself. So you are loosing pieces of the present to worry. What unfolds, will unfold."

I searched his previously inscrutable face and saw in it what he allowed me to see. The peace of one present moment. It was an offered gift which I took gratefully. The spell he had cast was broken by the clanging of the breakfast cart as it moved noisily down the hall. "I'll be back to check on you." I said.

"I'll try to be here." he answered cryptically.

I left his room thinking that I really needed another cup of coffee. I was loosing this battle of the tangible and felt the structure of my perceptions beginning to crumble. If I can just make it through my morning rounds, I told myself I'll be all right. Then it dawned on me that I seemed to be talking to myself a lot. Oh, would this morning never end!

Steadying myself, I went in to Sister Joachim's room. I was greeted there by a soft happy voice. "Good morning, dear. How are you today?"

"To tell you the truth, Sister, at this moment I'm not quite sure." I replied.

"Come and sit with me a minute, take a load off as they say." she giggled. I pulled a chair up to her bed and sat. I studied her face, and found it round and pink and serene. It spoke of a soft nature. What is happening to me, I thought? I am mesmerized by the messages of faces today!

"How is your neck?" I asked the smiling nun.

"It feels a little stiff, but this collar seems to help." she said. She went on to tell me about the last time that she had "sprained her neck" as she called it. My mind drifted, hearing her voice but concentrating on the peaceful countenance of her face. I believed that she had found something, something that has made her happy. One could see that just by looking at her face. This face that although decorated with wrinkles that spoke of living, seemed unused and new somehow.

The touch of her hand on my arm recalled me from my reflections. "I'm sorry Sister, what did you say?"

"Trust in the Lord to give you the answers that you seek my child."

"But Sister, not only am I having difficulty forming the questions I am not sure if there is someone beyond myself listening."

38

"The need to question is often the beginning of prayer." was her only reply. Saying that, she took my hand and gave it a gentle squeeze. And I was touched by her kind concern.

"Thank you, Sister, I better be on my way. I have to check on Father Bill and the Rabbis.

I left her room and entered the brightness of the hospital corridor, and was thankful for the familiarity of it. A couple of more stops and I've made it, I told myself. I stepped in to Father Bill's room only to find that it was empty. The bed was neatly made. And the only evidence that spoke of his occupancy was a worn black prayer book on the bedside stand. Great, now I've lost a priest! I chided myself. Just then I heard the murmur of male voices coming from the next room. Investigating I found that Father Bill had taken his breakfast tray in to the room of the Rabbis. He was sitting comfortably in the space between the two beds engrossed in conversation.

They did not see me at first, and not wanting to disturb them I quietly studied them. Father Bill was a big man dressed in clerical black. The Rabbis were slight of stature and looked like twins with matching beards and glasses. Each wore a skull cap on his head. They seemed to be earnestly arguing a point with the priest who sat consuming their words along with his breakfast. "Good morning." I said breaking in to their dialogue. Three faces turned towards the sound of my voice. The faces spoke of intelligence. These then were men who had grappled with the mysteries of this life and what lay beyond its boundaries. They had reached conclusions that they could live with, I thought with some envy.

"How are you all doing?" I asked.

"Fine." they answered in unison choir-like.

"Have you come to take the good priest away?" the Rabbi in the first bed joked. "He is lecturing us on Martin Buber and his fondness for the fourteenth century mystics." the second rabbi said. "And our food is getting cold."

"Don't mind them." the priest said. "They are mystics at heart, but will not concede the point." This started another course of discussion and they soon forgot that I was there. I left them thinking that they had found their God through study and contemplation, and wrapped in the comfort of their theology they did not feel the loneliness of the agnostic.

I made my way down the hospital corridor to the nursing station like some ship seeking a safe port after emerging through a storm. I wanted to be among things that I could understand. Concrete things like phones ringing off the hook, bins of charts and the petty squabbles that result from the dynamics of people brought together to do common work. Grounding things, anything that might distract me from what I had just experienced. But I could not erase their faces from

39

my memory. They danced before me bearing their separate messages. The message was, I believe, that each of us finds our own way to the center. Utilizing a philosophy or a religion, we seek the peace that that journey can bring. Some of us find it, and some of us do not. But we are all travelers, in some sense, on a pilgrimage that seeks something beyond ourselves to hang on to.

I really need another cup of coffee, I told myself. I checked my watch it was only 10 a.m., and I was exhausted.

Transgression

Uniforms, masks, gloves,
protective wear, and yet
if you let your guard
down, just a little,
they get past the barriers
and touch your heart.

The Wizard

I present you
with your pills,
like some conjurer
offering magic potions.

I think that I'll start
wearing a cape, and a
magician's hat.

Barriers

Two worlds,
two separate universes,
one on your side of the
bed rails, one on mine.

Give me your hand,
take strength.

No, I cannot let
the rails down.
Who then could
tell us apart?

Misnomer

Something is wrong.
There is nothing
hospitable about
the hospital.
We must either
change ourselves,
or it's name.

Degree of Separation

Sometimes you
are able to keep
your distance.
Sometimes you
are not.

Rescue

"Dr. Cart", "Code Blue",
announcements over the
P.A. system that someone
is trying to leave us, to
escape this "mortal toil".

The battle begins, chest
compressions, inhalations,
epinephrine, defibrillator
charged.

The outcome predestined
but, we don't give up.

Bound

We are connected
by the fragile
bonds of your needs.
Needs that once met
liberate you from
this place of sickness.
But I am left behind,
left to link up to
other needs again,
and again, and again.

Reprieve

Softly treading,
the night nurse rounds.
Down darkened sleeping
corridors she makes her way.
Respecting the fragile sleep
of those under her care.

Aware that, at least for
a few hours, it is the only
release from the bondage
of their illness.

Bereft

Hospital nights,
tangible, palpable
loneliness of
people sleeping
alone.
How unnatural!

Section Two

Patient Rhythms

Recovery is a lonely business.

Trapped

Wrapped in illness,
tightly bound, I
want to scream my
way to freedom.

Hunger

I miss the feel
of the wind, and
the warmth of the sun.
Like a lover, I yearn
for their touch.

Attempted Rescue

Friends drop in,
bringing with them
the outside world.
I am deeply touched
by their kindness,
by the time they take.
They serve as a link
to who I was before
this illness shaped
me to my present form.

Part of me connects,
is interested in what
they bring.
The rest of me is hiding
a million miles away,
beyond their reach.

Fallow

I am recovering ever so slowly.
It is nothing like I thought it
would be.
Endless days move to long nights
and I survive.
I have lost myself in this process
of healing.
And sense that something larger
than myself has taken over, directing
the flow of my energy.
I am as a ship tossed by waves
struggling to remain afloat.
And, on top of everything,
I have forgotten how to pray.

Families

OK, so my family wasn't perfect. And to some they might even seem a little strange. But they were all that was left on my mother's side, and since her death a year ago they hovered around me like protectors assigned to shield me from harm.

So I didn't find it odd that they decided to camp out at my bedside while I was in the hospital recuperating from orthopedic surgery. They would arrive midmorning armed with enough provisions to feed an army, and with magazines and books. They'd settle in, and with admirable vigilance observe the hospital staff that cared for me. At times taking notes or asking questions, they drove the nurses a little crazy. But their friendliness and quiet manner made them tolerable to all who came in contact with them. They would talk among themselves, endless prattle about family matters, friendly squabbles about trivial events, and often the comfortable soft drone of their voices put me to sleep. And when I awoke they were always there like guardian angels.

My father would call me on the phone and ask if those "damn insects" were still there. That is what he called them, "insects", "the bug family", "the pests". He said that if they were with me then he wasn't coming to visit. I was never quite sure what had happened between them that caused the rift, but I really didn't care. My mother had loved them dearly, and they she, and that was all that was important to me. Besides I liked having them around. They were an endless source of amusement and interest. Granted they were a tad unusual, but what family wasn't in some way.

They were four in number. Uncle Frank, my mother's brother, went through life sporting a beady little head that reminded you of a fly. He was bald, and had a thyroid problem that caused his eyes to bulge. His wife, my Aunt Ann, was skinny with spindly arms and legs. She always dressed in black, and seemed to be in perpetual motion, moving here and there, forever fussing with something, just like an ant. Their daughter Martha was moth-like. She was tall and slim with translucent skin and sandy hair that billowed out like moth wings. Her brother Benny was huge. And for some unknown reason he had a penchant for wearing black and yellow horizontally striped shirts that made him appear like a giant bumble bee. Benny was the one who always carried the flowers. I found that hilarious!

So that was why my father referred to them as "the insects". He often said that I should get a can of bug spray and "wipe the whole damn family out". But I didn't feel that way. I found them kind and considerate, and when you were with them you felt as if you were on an endless picnic.

On my third day in the hospital, I awoke from an evening nap and slowly opened my eyes. There was Benny in his bee shirt arranging the flowers, Aunt Ann with a piece of bread up to her mouth, cousin Martha reading close to the lamp, and Uncle Frank leaning against the wall. What a sight! My mother would have loved it so, and appreciated the unique picture that they presented. They sensed me wakening and began to flutter about. Fixing my pillows, straightening my blankets, and asking if I was all right. They bumped against each other in their zeal, and I thought what a lovely legacy they were. Gifts from my mother. And I also thought about how the beauty of them was lost to my father, who in his practicality was blinded to their uniqueness.

They grouped themselves in a half circle around my bed and told me that the doctor had come and had been sent away with instructions to return when I was awake. Uncle Frank said, with some annoyance, that my father had called, pretending to be an exterminator. "What's his problem, anyway?" he wanted to know. Martha told me that I had a new roommate. And then they all moved their chairs closer to the bed eager to tell me something.

"She's a dwarf." Martha said. "You know a little person." I looked towards the next bed, but the curtain was drawn obscuring my vision.

"She broke her leg." Uncle Frank continued. "They just brought her back from surgery."

"Her name is Violet." Aunty Ann added.

"And she has two sisters Rose and Dahlia." added Benny with suppressed glee.

I could hear the soft hum of female voices coming from behind the drawn curtain, and in the air was the sweet scent of flowers. Isn't life wonderful, I thought. Presenting us with its little ironical surprises! The flower family must have heard us talking because then I saw a small hand pulling back the curtain. Attached to the hand was a woman about four feet tall, dressed in red. "Hi, I'm Rose." she said. My family greeted her with warmth, and inquired after her sister. Rose drew the curtain further back, and in the bed was a little woman wearing a lavender bed jacket. "That's Violet," Rose said. "And that's our sister Dahlia." Dahlia sat on the other side of the bed, and was dressed in white. At first glance, seeing them grouped together like that, they brought to mind a small bouquet of flowers.

Rose said that Violet was still "groggy", but that the surgery had gone well. As I looked closer I saw that the cast immobilizing Violet's leg was green in color and made Violet resemble a flower with a broken stem. Rose was standing at Violet's side. And Benny noticed that there wasn't any place for her to sit, so he brought his chair over to where she was standing. Rose shyly thanked him. I was not sure, but I thought that I had seen something pass between them. Benny could not seem to take his eyes off of little Rose. And Rose, sensing this, blushed. Hmmm, this could prove interesting, I thought.

We sat in comfortable silence until a tall lean man in his twenties entered the room. Rose and Dahlia stood to greet him, and introduced him as Javier, their brother. He went over to Violet and touching her hand, recalled her from her post-surgical sleep. She smiled and said that she was OK, and that he was not to worry. Not convinced, he turned to his sisters for reassurance. While they talked, I noticed that cousin Martha had closed her book, and that she was watching the new arrival with some interest. Like a moth to a flame, I told myself. Aunty Ann also sensed that something was going on. Her eyes darted from Benny to Rose, and from Javier to Martha. They then settled on me and she winked. I glanced over to where Uncle Frank was leaning against the wall. He, on the other hand, appeared oblivious to what was unfolding.

Rose said that she was going down to the cafeteria for some coffee. She looked at Benny, who almost broke his neck trying to get around the bed fast enough, while saying that he could also use a cup of coffee. Javier's eyes rested on Martha as he said that he had not eaten all day, and that he would accompany them. Martha, reading the invitation in his eyes, also suddenly became eager for coffee. Dahlia said that she would stay behind in case Violet woke, and so the four of them filed out of the room.

Dahlia came over to our side of the room, and sat in the chair that Martha had vacated. I did not want to be impolite, but I was curious about Javier, about his Spanish looks and about his height as compared to his sisters. "Your brother has a beautiful name, and seems very nice." I said.

"Oh, he is our stepbrother." Dahlia said. "My father was married to a Spanish woman who died shortly after Javier was born." Hearing this Aunt Ann made a sympathetic sound and Uncle Frank inched his way along the wall closer to us. "A few years latter he met my mother, married, and we girls came along. He has been a loving brother, who has spent his life taking care of us, but I do wish that he would meet someone, someone with whom he could share his life."

Aunt Ann and I looked at each other with understanding. We also had similar hopes for our Martha.

Violet stirred, and called Dahlia's name. Dahlia slid off the chair and went to her. My aunt moved closer to me, and whispered with excitement. "Wouldn't it be grand if Martha and Javier got on, and if Rose liked Benny?"

"Now Annie, don't go jumpin the gun, they're just having coffee together." Uncle Frank said.

"But they've been gone for almost an hour." my aunt countered. "I think that it's more than just having coffee." I did not say anything. I was having too much fun. I thought that the uncoiling drama was almost worth the price of the surgery.

Now as they say, "Into each life a little rain must fall." Well, it was about to rain on our picnic big time! Because the next person to enter the room was my father. He clumped in to the room, briefly glancing at my aunt and uncle, saying, "Still here?" As he made his way over to me he caught site of Violet and Dahlia. He kissed my forehead and coarsely whispered, "What the hell is that?" while pointing his head in their direction. At this point, Uncle Frank slowly moved along the wall towards the girls, as my aunt reluctantly backed away from my side.

"That's Violet with the cast and one of her sisters Dahlia." I said with some defense in my voice. "Be quiet or they will hear you." I finished.

"I don't give a good God Damn if they do!" he retorted. "What is this a hospital or some kind of freak show?" he asked.

Although my father had always been good to me, he had this aggravating habit of breaking spells. He carried a coarse reality about him, and when you were with him his presence sought to dampen all thoughts of beauty. My mother used to say that it wasn't his fault. That he had led a difficult life. Working since early childhood, he had found little time to dream. My mother had been one of the few soft parts of his life, and now that she was gone he withdrew from the rest of the family in an attempt to protect himself from future losses. It was painful to watch, but I could not reach him. He had moved too far away.

"How ya doin kid?" he asked me.

"I'm fine Pa. Are you OK?"

"Yeah." was all that he said. We sat there in the silence that he had created.

I noticed that Uncle Frank was steadily moving himself along the wall towards the open door. My aunt kept staring at her retreating husband as if willing him not to flee. "I'll go and get the kids." he said. "I'm sure that they would like to see you, Phil," he continued as he almost choked on the lie that the words carried. With that he virtually flew out of the room, the growl coming from my father not fast enough to reach him. Aunt Ann was trapped and stayed frozen in the chair.

Just then we heard Violet crying. Soft petal-like sobs that touched the heart. Dahlia moved around the bed in some commotion trying to make her sister comfortable. "It's my leg Dahlia, the cast is so heavy that I can't move."

"I'll call the nurse." Dahlia said anxiously, as she pressed the call light. Violet attempted to get herself under control, but we could see that she was in pain. Ten minutes passed, and still no one came. Dahlia not able to see her sister suffer any longer, said that she was going to find a nurse.

"Wait a minute, wait a damn minute." my father said gruffly. "Let me see if I can help." If I hadn't been already laying down, I probably would have fallen. I was that surprised to see my father bother himself with concern for another. This indeed was interesting!

My father got up from his chair and went over to Violet. "You're all scrunched down." he said in a voice whose tone held what sounded like tenderness. "Hang on to me, and I'll pull you up." he continued. Violet, for some strange reason, trusting him draped her stem-like arms around his neck. And with one swift movement he lifted her towards the head of the bed. "There ya go, that should help you feel better." he said while adjusting the pillow under her head.

Violet reluctantly untangled her arms from him, and murmured, "Thanks, ever so much, the pain is gone now." My aunt and I looked at one another, and spoke with our eyebrows. She raised hers, and then I raised mine in response. We were communicating our disbelief about what we had just witnessed.

It wasn't that my father was a bad guy, it was just that he usually took great pains to separate himself from the needs of others. It was as if, when my mother died a year ago, he had buried himself with her. Entombing his emotions within the cement lined box that held her. Up to this minute I had held little hope of his return.

"Dahlia, Annie let's go down for some coffee, and let the girls take a rest." Saying that he came over to me and kissed my cheek with a kiss that held a lightness that I had not felt from him since before my mother took ill. It was a small thing really, but it held the promise of a beginning. My aunt and Dahlia followed him from the room, and I thought that sometimes people just needed to feel that they were necessary if even in the smallest of ways.

The room was quiet now, freed of the families. Violet was sleeping, and I lay there thinking about the day, and about our entwining families. I thought also about how each room in this hospital held a story, tales of concern, of love, of courage. Sometimes tinted with humor, sometimes colored by grief the unfurling sagas offered a glimpse in to the life of its bearer. If the walls could talk, I thought. What they had to say would deliver volumes, fill libraries. And when the patient is discharged from that room to home he carries his story with him leaving room for what the next has to tell.

Out of Reach

I keep staring
at the cross in
my room, and think
even He can't reach
the call light.

Spider Dance

A spider came to call.
I watched it move across
the wall, and envied its
mobility.

Samsara

Friends call, I say
that I am feeling like
myself again.
I don't tell them
that I have no idea
who emerged and who
did not.

Visibly Invisible

I watch the nurses
parading through my room,
doing things for me,
to me. And I long for
the feel of just one
touch signaling that
everything will be all
right, that they see me.
But they are too busy.

Vertical Healer

The doctor approaches.
I am at a horizontal
disadvantage.
He looms, only his
shadow touching me.
I wish that just once
he would sit down.

Communion

Cleaning ladies
fussing in my room,
surrogate mothers
arranging the sick
room.

They, not burdened
with the knowledge
of my illness, just
talk to me.

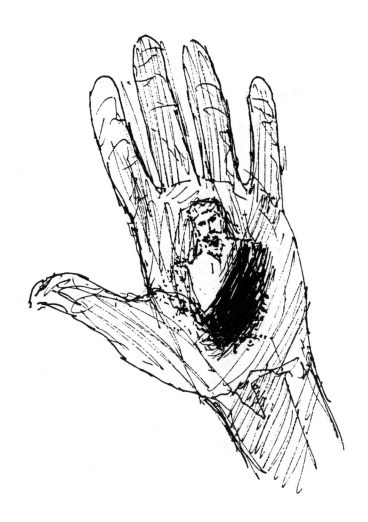

A Little Miracle

Sophie and Mabel were marvelous characters. Philosophers and missionaries disguised as cleaning women, they worked the night shift on a medical floor in our hospital. They were a comical pair dispensing solace and advice while mopping the floor, preaching "the word" while emptying the trash, and talking always talking in to the night.

Sophie was of Polish descent. She was a big woman, barely contained in her blue uniform. She had short white hair made shorter still by a tight perm that capped her head. Her face bore traces of the pretty girl she must have been, and she wore rhinestone glasses like they use to wear in the 1950's. She possessed the grace of a woman half her size and her deportment spoke of good breeding. She was like some dowager playing the part of a cleaning woman.

Mabel, Sophie's long time friend and coworker, was a mirror image of Sophie except that she was African American. She also strained the limits of the cloth that covered her. We used to joke that if their buttons ever popped, any one in their path would be fatally injured by the shear force of the projection. During the holidays, when food was plentiful on the unit, we were especially careful not to place ourselves in a position that would make us targets for these potential missiles.

While Mabel did not sport rhinestone glasses, she did possess a gold front tooth of which she was very proud. It was a gift she said from her now dead husband. A token of more bountiful times she flashed it generously when she smiled. Mabel wore her hair in a close nap that covered her skull and sculpted her head like the pictures you see of ancient African queens.

The two women, now in their sixties, had been friends since being paired at work twenty years ago. They had shared much, the loss of their husbands, troubles involving their children, and the toil of living in a high tech society that afforded them little opportunity for employment except for their housekeeping jobs. They took much pride in their work, and provided a comfortable, clean and homey environment for patients to grow well in and for us to work in.

Their cleaning carts were jammed with bottles of mysterious fluids and mops and brushes and multicolored rags. Both women were religious, and on their carts in one of the corners they had created an altar-like area with a picture of their savior

Jesus. Sophie's Jesus was white with a glowing face and a blue robe. Mabel's Jesus was dark skinned and wore an African shirt. Before each picture stood a plastic votive candle whose light was battery operated and swirled when lit casting dancing lights over the walls. I came across them once in the room of a dying patient. Fake candles ablaze catching the rhinestones in Sophie's glasses and bouncing against Mabel's gold tooth. It was a spectacular sight in its own right rivaling the pageantry of many a cathedral.

Sophie and Mabel believed that it was their mission, their calling to be at the side of those dying alone. Many a lonely soul left this life flanked by these two kind strangers and their make shift altars. In the early years the hospital chaplain was a little put out with their zeal, and once in an uncharitable moment he complained to their supervisor that perhaps the women were overstepping themselves. When the super sought them out that night he could find nothing wrong with their carts. Because Sophie and Mabel had placed an inverted water pitcher over their altars. Wearing a look of complete innocence they listened to the admonitions of their boss, and when he went away they lifted the pitchers liberating their shrines, and were back in business again. The chaplain, recognizing the futility of the situation, choose to compromise and elicited a promise from the women that included a phone call to him before they struck out to position themselves at death's door. All three were happy with this arrangement that made them teammates, so to speak, in this special facet of hospital ministry. Once in a great while there was a stray relative who witnessed the ministrations of Sophie and Mabel. Some would write the hospital administrators thanking them for their concern and special treatment. The administrators, of course, had no idea what they were talking about, and chalked it up to the ramblings of grief.

The women never forced their services on anyone, but choose instead to minister to that lone patient meeting death without the benefit of family or friends. Sophie and Mabel would sit on the periphery as report was given at the shift change and gather potential souls. If they discovered that one of their charges was as Mabel used to say "one of them eggnostics", they'd hide their Jesus under the water pitcher so as not to offend and just keep the person company as they made their way in to the next life.

Their busiest time was pneumonia season when casualties of that illness were admitted for antibiotics and hydration. The usually frail and elderly victims lay exhausted in their beds, and Sophie and Mabel could be found offering sips of water or placing cold compresses on their fevered brows while cleaning the sick room. And if one of the patients died, they'd accompany the morgue cart to the elevator. Their carts positioned one on each side of the newly departed, fake candles glowing they would proceed with all the solemnity of a state funeral.

And so went life on the unit. Seasons flowed, patients came and were cared for, and Sophie and Mabel were always there ministering and cleaning. Then one day, uncharacteristically, Mabel did not show up for work. Sophie was beside herself with worry. She tried to phone Mabel several times, and receiving no answer grew frantic. She convinced one of the orderlies to walk over to Mabel's apartment during his dinner break. Her worse fears were confirmed when he called her from Mabel's saying that it looked like Mabel had suffered a stroke and that he had called 911 and that she should be arriving at the emergency room any minute. Sophie dropped the phone, and moving as fast as her big frame would allow made for the stairs. She stopped before Mabel's cart and picked up the picture of the black Jesus and carefully tucked it in to her pocket.

When she arrived in the emergency room Mabel was already in a cubicle surrounded by a flurry of activity. Someone was taking her blood pressure, someone else was hanging an intravenous bag, and one of the doctors was shining a light in Mabel's eyes. They stopped for a brief time when they saw Sophie and parted to allow her room at her friend's side. Sophie forced a smile to her face and gripping the limp hand of Mabel tried not to cry. Mabel could not speak with her voice, but her eyes said much. In them Sophie read the fear that Mabel felt. Her mouth drooped some exposing the gold tooth, and a tear escaped her eye. The activity continued around them, but Sophie held on to Mabel's hand like a life line to another world.

The doctor was saying that they were going to send Mabel for a scan of her head. Sophie remembered the picture of Mabel's black Jesus in her pocket. She gently removed it and placed it in front of Mabel's face. Mabel stared at the picture in prayer, and then thanked Sophie with her eyes. Sophie placed the picture in Mabel's good hand, and watched as her friend gripped it tightly. Sophie felt an arm around her shoulder and saw the chaplain standing at her side. She held up till they moved Mabel down the hall to x-ray, and then she began to sob heartbreaking sounds that were muffled by the chaplain's chest. The chaplain knowing that words were futile just held her in silence.

Meanwhile, in the x-ray department they were rolling Mabel in to the scanning tube, Mabel clutched her Lord's picture even tighter, and felt a warmth in her hand that soothed her. She prayed deep prayers, petitions begging a recovery that would not make her a burden to anyone. Exhausted, she gave herself up to a power larger than herself, and drifted in to a heavy sleep.

The story of Mabel's stroke spread throughout the hospital troubling her coworkers. Many said silent prayers as they went about their work and waited for some news of her condition. The nurses on Mabel's floor prepared her room with tender care as one would for a special guest. And Sophie and the chaplain waited in the emergency room for her return. Mabel's doctor sought them out after reading the scans, and in encouraging tones told them that things were not as bad as he had feared, but that it was still too early to tell how things would resolve. He went on to explain in technical terms about the bleed in her brain. Sophie tried to listen to what he was saying, but all she really heard was the hope in his voice, and she held on to its promise. Sophie looked beyond the doctor and saw that they were wheeling Mabel towards the elevator. She pumped the doctor's hand with thanks and went to her friend.

Mabel lay flat on the cart, her eyes were opened and she studied the ceiling noting some dirty patches. Sophie appeared, her large frame blocking the light eclipse-like. Mabel saw the worry written on her friend's face and tried to console her, but no words made it over her lips. Although she was frightened, and felt like a prisoner in her body, she thought that somehow she would be all right. She didn't question where the feeling came from, she just trusted it and held on to the picture of her Jesus for dear life.

When Mabel arrived in her room she was transferred to the waiting bed with care. Her eyes darted over the down turned faces, and she took comfort from the concern she saw. And then the tiredness over took her again and she escaped in to the deepest of sleeps. Her dreams contained her life. Family members, long dead, visited her bearing large bouquets of flowers each petal somehow a prayer for her recovery. Her husband came and shined the gold tooth, and then kissed her forehead as he used to do when returning home from work. No language was spoken. All paraded in and out of her dreams in a peaceful silence. In one sequence Sophie appeared, the rhinestones in her out dated glasses aglow with beams of light that somehow urged Mabel to awaken. But Mabel wanted to stay where she was, entombed in the quiet safe place that held her motionless. In the end it was the rays from Sophie's glasses that pulled her back forcing her to awaken against her will.

She awoke to the murmur of excited voices. She thought at first that she was dead, but then felt an ache in her old back that she didn't think the dead could feel. Mabel heard her name being called over and over again, and thought, "What in the good Lord's name is all the fuss about, I'm right here." "Hello". she loudly said. And then cried with joy at the sound of her own voice. Startled by the sound of her, those circling her bed transferred their attention to her face. "What time is it?" she asked.

"It's one o'clock in the afternoon." one of the nurses replied.

"Oh my, I've lost a whole day.". Mabel replied. She did not understand the silence that followed her reply. Those around her stood mute. She wondered what was wrong with everyone. Sophie came forward and touching Mabel's arm said

69

gently, "My dear old friend, you had a stroke two weeks ago. You have been asleep since that time. Today was to be the day that the doctors decided what should be done."

Mabel looked in to Sophie's face and tried to understand what the words meant.

"You mean you all thought that I was a goner?" she said clumsily, not used to making sounds. "But I was just sleeping and dreaming the most wonderful dreams. And now I feel strong and well again." Saying that she moved her arms towards her head, testing her new found strength. She was surprised when Sophie stopped the progress of her right arm.

"Mabel there is something else that we need to tell you, well, show you really." Sophie then took Mabel's right hand, and gently opening her fist exposed Mabel's palm. Mabel stared and stared not trusting what she was seeing. "Now don't be frightened Mabel." Sophie urged. "We can't explain it, we don't know how it happened ..." The rest of what Sophie said was lost to Mabel because with all of the concentration that she could muster she was trying to comprehend what she saw. On her palm, smudged somewhat, was the face of Jesus. It was the same face found on her holy card.

Mabel's doctor, quiet up till now, spoke saying that the image could have been absorbed from the picture that Mabel had so tightly held the first few hours after her stroke. He spoke of dyes from the card and the heat from Mabel's hand and the chemical reaction that might have occurred causing a transference of the icon to Mabel's hand. Mabel heard his words, but did not give them much credence. She knew that this was a little miracle, a sign that she would heal and grow strong, and she was so thankful for this gift of recovery. The doctor was still talking, saying that the image would probably soon wear off. But Mabel knew that even if that were so, the memory of it would never fade from her heart. So Mabel listened politely and nodded her head, placating her doctor. He would have to find his own miracle, she thought. And she was not about to let him explain hers away.

"We should let you rest now." one of the nurses said. Those surrounding her bed took the hint and reluctantly began to leave. As the room cleared Mabel smiled the biggest smile exhibiting her gold tooth. For in one corner of the room was Sophie's cart, fake candle gleaming beacon-like, the swirling rays falling over the two friends.

"I guess its safe for me to move my cart now." Sophie said.

"I'm gonna be just fine now Soph," Mabel said. "To tell you the truth, I wasn't sure till I saw this here picture on my hand," she continued. "It gave me hope, made me feel like going on, like I had a chance to make it." The two woman looked at Mabel's palm, and then said a prayer of thanks.

Sophie noticed that Mabel looked worn and ready for sleep. "I'll be back tonight, dear, why not try and get some rest." she said. Mabel's eyes closed and her breath moved her chest in a peaceful rhythm. Sophie thought that it was safe to leave and maneuvered her cart to the door. As she left the room, the corner of the cart bumped the door, dumping the contents of a small basket on the floor. Sophie glanced at Mabel nervously, but then relaxed as she saw that Mabel was still sleeping. She knelt on the floor and gathered the little bottles of dye and tiny paint brushes and placed them back in the basket.

One might ask what is a miracle anyway? And one might answer that perhaps friendship is the greatest miracle of all. One might, you know!

Genesis

Slowly my spirit returns,
and I remember what it was to feel like
myself again.
Where did I go, and how in
the world did I ever find
my way back?

Hope

Early light
on morning leaves,
a beginning.

Painted Illusions

How do we differ,
tell me?
From that misguided
bird, that throws
itself against a
window, having lost
the ability to
distinguish the illusion of sky
painted there.

Are we both not
stunned to discover
that all was not
what it seemed?

Query

These rails
around my bed.
Do they keep
me in, or you
out?

Moon Nurses

I lay in this hospital bed,
and wait for the "Moon Nurses"
to appear.

Those nurses of the night,
tricking their body clocks
in to thinking that it is day.

They enter our rooms
as our mother's once did.
Checking to see that we are
all right.

Their presence making the night a little
less frightening.
The "Moon Nurses".

The Mask

I can't get this patient
mask off my face.
Its stuck there, obliterating
who I really am.

I grab its edges with the
the little strength that
I have left, and attempt
to pull it from me.

I hear the humble pleas
for service that escape
over its painted mouth,
and I almost choke on the
bountiful "please" and
"thank yous".

It stifles my anger, affords me no outlet
to express the rage
that I feel at what is
happening to me.

My tears well up
beneath the mask, and
I think that I will drown
if it is not dislodged.

I lay still, and from
under the mask search
for the tiniest crack,
the smallest of openings
from which I might emerge!

The Need to Center

Beyond ourselves,
farther than the eye can see,
there sits a healing power.

Distracted and estranged
from its energy we flounder
in our infirmity.

Tossed and blocked
by fear and pain we've
misplaced the capacity
to rejuvenate.

Because, you see,
beyond ourselves farther
than the eye can see,
there sits we.

Deprivation

My senses
are offended
by the sterility
of the hospital room.

No comfortable smells.
No soothing sounds.

Everything feels harsh.
And the white brightness
of the hospital sheets
hurt my eyes.

Will someone please
just get me out of here,
so that I can get better.

Detached

It is the loneliness
of illness that pains
the most.

Surrounded by loved ones
and friends, one still somehow
remains alone, adrift.

Why is that?

Ailing Poets

We are all perhaps
afflicted poets.
Searching for a rhythm
with which we might
define ourselves.
Some strain on which
we can ride.
But sickness sings
no song. No merry
tune anyway, and we
are left muted with
no outlet for our voice.

Platitudes

"Don't give up."
"Hang in there."
"You'll be fine."

The "Plats", as I
call them, spoken with
good intentions bounce
against me. Deflected
by this armor of illness.

Pretty words made palatable
by the kindness that rides
behind them.

They trespass across
the bed rails, lacking
conviction once freed
from the speaker's lips.

I listen intently, and try
to force my face in to an
acceptable expression, not
wanting to offend the giver
or the gift.

Succor

My love,
I am unable to
make any of this
easier for you.

I stand helpless,
the barrier of your
illness keeping us
apart.

This is a personal
battle, the fight
of your life.
And I see how the
struggle weakens you.

My love,
I am unable to make any of this
easier for you.
But I am here
at your side.

Deserted

I feel like
some abandoned
parachutist tethered
to these IV lines.
Waiting for rescuers
that never come.

Georgie

So, here I am laying in this hospital bed recovering from hip surgery, feeling lonely and sorry for myself. My attention span is that of a gnat, and I'm trying to link thoughts together to make some sense of my predicament. I lift my head and examine my trussed up leg which is immobilized by some kind of high tech orthopedic paraphernalia. I stare at the injured leg and I wonder if I will ever walk again or dance again. I don't dance much really. But I'd like to think that I could if I wanted to. I watch the door fearing that someone will enter that wants to move me, and I think that I will kill anyone that tries. Weak from the surgery, barely able to hold the water glass, I decide that I'll feign sleep instead, play possum, if someone comes in. Let them work for their money I conclude. These are the thoughts that pass through my mind, and I urge myself to get a grip, get the old bean working again, think about something other than myself and the pain that is beginning to grow in my leg. And I decide to give it, my brain, some exercise. I force it to remember. Its a game I play sometimes, traveling back in time challenging the release of stored up experiences to come forth and be examined. I call it brain jogging. And suddenly I am back in the third grade and from the neurotic folds of my mind there materializes Georgie.

Georgie, perhaps working out some karmic debt, was born to simple minded parents. He resembled the Hunchback of Notre Dame, without the hunchback. His shoulders were stooped, probably sloped from the burdensome weight of the life that was dealt to him. In the 1950's he was labeled as "retarded". Even as a kid he looked like an old man. He shuffled as he walked, had arms and legs that never seemed to do what he wanted, and possessed a huge bumpy face. His eyes spoke of being trapped and wounded. His speech was clogged and sometimes guttural, and his voice held a pain that was too complicated for the rest of us kids to understand. One wonders what transgressions he could have possibly committed in a previous existence that resulted in the sentence of his life.

Georgie wore gray work pants like my father used to wear. A rope belt circled his waist, probably tied by his mother or by his moronic father, because I don't think that Georgie could have managed that simple task. He was usually dirty except for his face. And when I think about the effort it must have taken for this small act of grooming it breaks my heart. What did he think as he washed over the lumpy face that was his? Did he know that he was different, damaged? Did he own the capacity to envy? I hope not. Not even the gods could be that cruel.

Georgie lived on my block, on the other side of the street, some houses down. It was a blue collar neighborhood, kept clean by mothers and grandmothers granted the luxury of staying home. The era before women were shorn from their children and gobbled up and sacrificed in the work force. Georgie's house was run down and broken like Georgie and his family. It screamed for intervention, but in those days and in my neighborhood everybody minded their own business. It was a time when we shunned things different from ourselves. A time before social workers were popular and whispers of child abuse were kept secret. We all just sort of closed our eyes and pretended that we didn't see the pain and need on Georgie's face. I think now, that I will never forgive myself for missing acts of kindness, but I was just a little girl without much understanding of the world in which I found myself.

I hear someone entering the room, and with eyes full of tears I shut the memories of Georgie's life down. It takes me but a minute to fake an unconscious state, hoping that the intruder will leave. I keep my eyes shut against the sight of them. I hear something being placed on the bedside table, and waiting a safe minute I slowly open one eye and catch a glimpse of a hospital volunteer exiting the room. On the table is a lovely bouquet of fall flowers with a card wishing me well. The card is fashioned in the shape of a pumpkin and reminds me of Halloween, and that brings me back to Georgie.

Most of the kids I knew began in October to dream of our favorite holiday Christmas. But I do not think that that was so for Georgie. I'm just assuming now, mind you, but I wonder what he could have possibly wished for or expected. It's almost to painful to consider. I do remember, however, that he seemed to take great joy in Halloween. He walked around days before the 31st of October, with a pirate scarf over his lumpy head and a patch covering one eye. He carried a stick that I guess was supposed to be a sword and an old brown bag that held his candy. He walked among us this one night of the year without fear of being assailed. Halloween, a night of freaks and goblins all of us covered in costumes that hid our identity. Maybe Georgie didn't feel so different on that day, and maybe that was why he was so happy. The gods had granted him this one night, this small piece of happiness.

I try to shift my weight in the bed. I'm restless with all this remembering, but I can't seem to stop once the Georgie gates are opened. Unable to halt the childhood images that flow freely now the next thing that I remember is Georgie standing in the schoolroom at the black board with the other boys. The nun, a real witch, had placed some kind of math problem on the board, and was chastising the boys for not being able to figure them out. Georgie, I remember, was at the side board holding a piece of chalk in his hand. He probably had difficulty understanding what the chalk did, let alone being able to figure out a math problem. I recall the nun approaching him and then her banging his head against the board. Georgie's face held surprise. Expecting him to do the math was as outlandish as requiring him to explain the theory of relativity. I wonder now, why she could not see that. The room was silent I remember, we on some level I know, I must believe, felt some sympathy for Georgie, but little cowards that we were, we kept silent. She banged his head again and again, and remembering the look on his face I see that his soul was farther advanced than hers would ever be. But I am unable to put the anger aside that I felt, still feel towards her, these forty some years latter.

One of the last memories of Georgie that I own was our First Communion day. I can still picture him packaged in a shiny dark blue suit and a crumpled white shirt. The choir was singing as we marched up the church aisle. Georgie had been drilled by the nuns to follow the boys in front of him and to open his mouth to accept the holy wafer. Perhaps not wanting to make a mistake, he kept his mouth opened as he shuffled down the aisle. Or perhaps he just couldn't remember two things so he made them one. Some that saw him snickered. But Georgie just kept his mouth open and when the priest finally placed the wafer in Georgie's mouth he closed it tenderly around the form of a god that had treated him so cruelly.

In those simple times, when we were taught to trust a god who could be invited in to our lives with a prayer. I began to doubt my faith. I figured that Jesus, who could raise the dead and heal the lepers, should have done more for Georgie. And I was disappointed in his performance and in his neglect of this needy boy. It wasn't till some thirty years latter that the embers of faith began to flicker in me again, fanned by my own need to connect with something beyond myself.

I will myself to stop thinking about Georgie, just for a minute. I stare at the ceiling and then let my eyes travel over the walls to the door, hoping that someone will enter and grant me a reprieve from these painful memories. But no one appears, and so I try to move my leg and it feels like it weighs a hundred pounds and I'm sure that I'll never walk again. I say a prayer for my recovery and then I laugh because I'm granted this piece of insight which shows me how far I have traveled from the third grade, which isn't far at all. Pathetic, isn't it?

So, back to Georgie. I tell myself let's finish this, get it over with, all the while cursing myself for starting all this in the first place. I try very hard to remember when the last time was that I recall Georgie. But I am unable to place him past the third grade. A vague memory begins to surface. I see Georgie's face beyond the dirty window of his house, watching me as I walk to school. I see him raise his hand in a clumsy greeting, and with horror I watch the little girl that I was turn from him. I'm crying now, and I believe that even if I spend the rest of my life doing good works, I shall never atone for that one act of cruelty so many years ago. You the reader of this tale, might think that I am being overly dramatic, and too sensitive. But one day you will remember something similar in your life. Some time when you were less than the gods designed, and then you will understand how I feel.

In this hospital bed, with only myself and memories for company. I am astounded at the clarity with which I recall Georgie. That events from forty years ago could hold such power amazes me. Dim recollections of childhood friends parade before me, then fade. But Georgie stands bright and clear demanding inspection and reflection. That simple, pathetic boy it seems possessed a power so great that he still lives to teach me something about myself and about my treatment of others. The memory of him urges me to be a better person, to be more sympathetic, to be kinder. Perhaps the gods do know what they are doing after all, and we are all not just cast upon this earth in a chaotic fashion, charged to find our own way. Perhaps we are expected to rise to the heights of our potential and become more "godlike" ourselves. Perhaps.

The Georgie memories grow quieter now, having left their mark. I try to turn in the bed, but I am stopped by my surgerized leg. Frustrated I grab the bar over the bed and attempt to pull myself up. The door opens and in to the room cautiously enters a young man delivering newspapers. He wears a simple expression on his face. His ears are huge flaps attached to the side of his head. His hair is plastered down to one side, and he sports a crooked bow tie. He stutters, can't quite seem to get the word *n-e-wsp-a-aper* out. I look in to his eyes, and see some kin to Georgie there. Given another chance, I smile the biggest smile that I can muster and say. "Hey, how are you doing? Come on in, I've been waiting for you!"

Lorn

"Eli, Eli,
lema sabacthani."

See, even the Christ
once felt forsaken.
Take Heart!

Jagged

RHYTHMS